THE EAST WIND BLOWS WEST

THE EAST WIND
BLOWS WEST

New and Selected Poems by

George Jonas

Selected & Introduced by Barbara Amiel
Afterword by J. Michael Yates

CACANADADADA

THE EAST WIND BLOWS WEST
Copyright © 1993 George Jonas

CACANADADADA PRESS LTD.
3350 West 21st Avenue
Vancouver, B.C. Canada
V6S 1G7

Set in Baskerville 11 pt on 13½
Typesetting: The Typeworks, Vancouver, B.C.
Printing: Hignell Printing, Winnipeg, Manitoba
Cover Design: Cecilia Jang
Author Photo: Linda Corbell

The publisher wishes to thank the Canada Council and the British Columbia Cultural Services Branch for their generous financial assistance.

CANADIAN CATALOGUING IN PUBLICATION DATA

Jonas, George, 1935–
    The east wind blows west

    ISBN 0-921870-08-6
    I. Title.
PS8519.O53E2 1993   C811'.54   C92-091470-5
PR9199.3.J65E2 1993

ACKNOWLEDGEMENTS

George Jonas's poetry has appeared in the following periodicals and books: *Contemporary Literature in Translation, Expanding Horizons* (McGraw Hill), *Kayak, Made in Canada* (Oberon Press), *Modern Canadian Verse* (Oxford), *New American and Canadian Poetry* (Beacon Press), *New Wave Canada* (Contact Press), *Notes for a Native Land* (Oberon Press), *PRISM international, Quarry, Queen's Quarterly, Saturday Night, Saturday Review, The Blasted Pine* (Macmillan), *The Canadian Forum, The Malahat Review, The New Romans* (M. Hurtig), *The Penguin Book of Canadian Verse, The Tamarack Review, Thumbprints* (Peter Martin Associates), and on the CBC radio program "Anthology."

ALSO BY GEORGE JONAS

The Absolute Smile (Anansi, 1967)

The Happy Hungry Man (Anansi, 1970)

Cities (Anansi, 1973)

By Persons Unknown: The Strange Death of Christine Demeter
    (with Barbara Amiel; Macmillan, 1977)

Pushkin (New Canadian Drama—1, Borealis, 1980)

Final Decree (Macmillan, 1981)

The Scales of Justice, Vol. 1 (CBC Enterprises/Macmillan,
    1983)

Vengeance: The True Story of an Israeli Counter-Terrorist Team
    (Lester & Orpen Dennys/Collins, 1984)

The Scales of Justice, Vol. 2 (CBC Enterprises/Lester & Orpen
    Dennys, 1986)

Crocodiles in the Bathtub (Collins, 1987)

Greenspan, The Case for the Defense (with Edward L.
    Greenspan; Macmillan, 1987)

A Passion Observed (Macmillan, 1989)

Politically Incorrect (Lester Publishing, 1991)

CONTENTS

New Poems

FOREWORD

I first encountered the poetry of George Jonas in a Canadian Broadcasting Corporation elevator. One autumn day in 1967, a couple of CBC executives going to the second floor of Toronto's Maitland Street building looked curiously at me, and one of them said: "I've just been reading about you." They had a copy of *The Absolute Smile* in their hands.

We were friends then, George Jonas and I, not yet lovers and a long way from the husband and wife we would become until our divorce in 1979. I knew very little of his poetry, had read none of the poems of which they spoke, and only read *The Absolute Smile* later that week with the casual narcissism of a 25-year-old.

Two years later when I was living in a different country, in touch with Jonas only every six months or so, I read the book again. The first poem I read was "Five Stanzas on Perfection" and I was hooked. That poem gave me a hint of what the arts at their best can offer—a moment where something beyond one's own ordinary reach is glimpsed and the darkness makes a bit of sense. It's like a flash of lightning, I suppose, illuminating an unknown mental landscape. I've been an addict of Jonas's poetry ever since and only lament that there are so few new poems these days.

This potted history of my acquaintance with Jonas and his poems is an indulgence but necessary. Though there is a strong literary tradition of spouses, or those involved in close relationship with an author, writing biographies or books of critical analysis on their work and selecting anthologies, in Canada my professional commentaries on Jonas's work have sometimes been greeted with scepticism, a yawn, and "... well, she would say that, wouldn't she?"

Truth is, she wouldn't. I have liked the writings of a number of people I wouldn't dream of dating and have dated a number of people whose writing had no appeal to me at all. In that respect, my critical faculty and my emotional life simply don't intermingle.

This anthology is an idiosyncratic choice but a few threads do inform the selection. Poetry is damnably difficult to write and a reputation can be made on two or three brilliant poems, but not if you only write two or three. A poet has to present a body of work to be taken seriously and those exquisite verses—the cushion-cut VVVS1 diamonds—sparkle among a setting of worthy but less perfect stones. In this collection there are at least a couple of dozen poems that give me what Arthur Koestler called the "Ah!" factor. Readers will choose their own, I expect, but mine include "Kunsthistorisches Museum," "Landmarks" and "Going Home" from *Cities* (1973) and perhaps "A Bench in the Park" (from *The Happy Hungry Man*).

Other poems are chosen because of the light they shed on the author and his psyche. An author has to have a hell of an interesting psyche to get me curious about it and I think Jonas has. Not surprisingly, he wrote more often about himself in the earlier books of poetry, when he was a younger man. Later on, grown-up and grown-out of some of the more obvious existential fears that life under totalitarian regimes in Budapest and his subsequent status as a Hungarian refugee in Canada produced, he explored other themes.

Increasingly those themes were political and they shed a remarkable light on the nature of tyranny and the paradoxes of liberty. The narrative of "Hotel Royal" and the two "Emile X" poems (*Cities*) give me more sense of the moral consequences of the most monstrous tyranny history has seen than any number of the academic tomes now being published. As for a poem like "Air Raid Rhymes," well, I can only cry: lucky enough to be born in England during the Second World War, I had no notion of what it must have been like to be a Jewish child in Budapest in 1944, living under bombardment by the Allies, siege by the Russians and the murderous rampages of the Hungarian Nazis.

But Jonas is not a "Jewish" poet, a "Hungarian" poet or even a political poet. Pigeonholing him misses the point. He can be a storyteller as in the poem "Airport"; he is a polemical poet as in "White Anglo-Saxon Protestant in Central Park" (*Cities*) or "That's Not the Way the World Works" from *The Happy Hungry Man* (1970). Actually, Jonas and I have always felt differently about his "polemical" poems—he tends to be less interested in them than I am. Perhaps that is because like most Westerners I am fascinated by what it must have been like to live under tyranny and love the way his work dissects it, while Jonas is simply relieved that he survived it.

Ultimately, for me the finest poem in this anthology is neither a polemic nor a political work but rather the new poem "Nocturnal," which is a lyrical poem. This reinforces my view that in the end, Jonas belongs to no school and fits no category. "I don't know what originality is," he once told me as we sat listening to some poets reading their version of Black Mountain poems, "but it is no more original to imitate current fashions than it is to imitate Tennyson." That recognition has kept his work out of all the blind alleys into which a preoccupation with such matters as technique or formalism could lead him.

So here they are. My selection. These poems have entertained me, soothed me, inspired and delighted. I can't imagine a world without ideas and music and moral truths and so I can't imagine it without the poetry of George Jonas.

Barbara Amiel
London, April 1992

from THE ABSOLUTE SMILE

INTRODUCTION

The absolute smile of our little-known Lord
Immerses the world by day in its light
And all hostilities stay undeclared
In the brush or shallow water of the night.

The inviting pink of the dawn's open mouth
Turns to well-bred shades of frozen blue later
But it is in the soft shadows of twilight that things mate,
Call out in undertones and reconnoitre.

And my two-bedroom apartment floats on such waves
Of the established and well-made universe
That God rings my doorbell, approves of my rich loves,
And tells me those I hate could not be any worse.

Easy to hurt by silence and by sound
I, as most men, increasing and alone
Grow horrible, and search in my wound,
From live trees cut a crutch on which to lean.

Springs are incidental to what I have become
And winters affect me not at all:
I keep alive by breathing and in some
Ways I resemble myself even more.

I murder in the inside darkness, I
Have learned to slice an apple and not touch it;
The universe recedes in disarray
I sit in metal towers and I watch it.

But I'm making a note of things I do not like
And I do not like anything. Today
The notes are multiplying in my scroll of black
You are in it, so is she, so am I.

PEACE

I wish to make a positive statement
Of happy hunters returning from the woods.
Wardens of dwindling flocks, serious concern
Dwells in their moist and beautiful eyes.

There is no conflict that love or bullets
Could not resolve in time.
Gardens are carefully planned. Long rows of roses sit
In all directions around any house.

There is always a period of peace
Between two blows, when a smiling landscape
Surrounds with blue light the resting warrior.
The raised arm hardly shows among the ferns.

At such times rabbits jump out of their trenches
And stand listening at the entrance of the field.
Worms pop out of the ground in open amazement,
Sharp-beaked birds freeze unfalling in their dive.

The moment is guarded by dustbins along the streets
Of low and crippled suburbs where later
Children come out of hiding and women pause for breath.
Hate, suspended, sways gently back and forth.

Rats are pacing the floor, thinking,
A loaf of bread cuts itself into warm slices,
A glass of milk travels to India,
Warships lean on their guns and close their eyes.

The beauty of such moments is hardly useful
Except for the purpose of missing a heartbeat,
As old men sit at tables, ready to talk.
For there is nothing to talk about.

IN ANY CITY

In any city at any hour of the day
We pray.

With narrow, calculating eyes
We are getting off streetcars in front of churches.
Not too far from stock markets and parliament buildings
We attempt to placate God
By giving pieces of candy to filthy children.
Generally
For each ten men we destroy
We restore one;
For each dollar we extort
We return a nickel to the priest
And a penny to the poor.

Luckily our God is a Jew
A shrewd kindly old Jew who knows his children well.
Our way of doing business is his way.
His motto too is live and let live
And a little honest profit is all he expects
On which to keep his Kingdom going.
A slight depression now and then cannot be avoided
In his difficult line.
If he can make us do our bit
And be in some vague fear of him all the time
He is satisfied
And in the end he opens for us
The gates of his heaven.

Of course, there will be a few even he cannot help.
A few who are unable to find a place in this soap opera of a
        world
Misfits, who are not at home, no matter what,
In this fat, happy, cause-and-effect, give-and-take universe,
A few vicious saints who want all or nothing.

These lost souls are out of the reach of God.
He cannot give them all because he too has to stay in
        business
So he gives them nothing.
With a sad flick of his beautiful patriarchal finger
He sends them flying after a while
Into the outer darkness.

ONCE MORE

Kirov was shot, Solon will rot in jail,
even the smallest hold-up man will hang,
Eichmann has died seven times, but the real,
the real murderers all live in my street.

They go to work each day at eight o'clock.
Some take the bus, some drive, and many walk.
They have a child or two, they like a smoke,
their wives wear rings, Sunday they cut the grass.

They talk about the business, the weather,
there is a faint click as they lock the door.
Only a few of them would hurt a fly
and all of them support a family.

Will they be caught? Is theirs the perfect crime?
All I see is the circle of the time,
all I know is I have to be prepared.

Caution causes me to glide through the walls
at night and stand beside them just to see
how long they have to wash their hands before
they turn the light out and they go to sleep.

TUESDAY, JUNE 28

I wonder if there will be room for both of us
In this poem.

I have explored you as far as my fingers would take me
And you are nowhere.
Perhaps you invite so lightly
Their expedition through your body's regions
Because you know:
Fingers can't reach you.

Aimlessly, like an iceberg
You float on
With most of what you are immersed
In jealous depths of yourself
A tip above the surface showing
To photograph, to dress and to destroy.

I will stop searching for you, I will
Pretend that I have found you: you are
Easy enough to see, to feel, to touch.
I will allow your tongue to flicker
In and out of my ear, your lip
To circle my lap, and not remember
You are only doing your duty and have no hope
Of pleasing even yourself.

I will stay with you
Until the wind blows you away.

Whenever we meet
After our ritual is over
I will incline my head and listen
For the silence between your breasts.

EXIT LINES

At present I still have
A choice of deaths,
I could, for example, die of a difficult disease
For medical science and I could
Die for a stranger who has never learned to swim.
I could also die for the Queen.
These are quite honourable deaths
But they don't appeal to me.
I think I'll die for Barbara.
Strangers are strangers
Whether they can swim or not
Barbara is a friend.
Medical science
Requires long hours, depressing nights
In hospitals, syringes and white towels
For Barbara I could die with my clothes on.
The Queen, lovely as she is,
Has no breasts to compare with Barbara's
And I have never kissed the Queen's throat.
It makes sense for me to die for Barbara.

TEMPORAL

This is one of those Tuesdays
I want to be old.
Then you will be old too
For I wish you a long, long life.

Sometimes I will see you in the street
As I see other old women now
Who used to be desperately desired
By all sorts of old, dead men.
It is a comfort for me to see them
And oh, it will be a comfort for me to see you.
Grey strands of crinkly hair half-hiding
Long, flat ears
Thin legs ending in knotted ankles
Shuffling in black walking shoes
A quick glance at you
From top to bottom
That's all.

If doctors still permit me the odd cigar
I will light one after each such meeting
And sit by a window overlooking a street
A crowded street, full of young, nervous girls
Hurrying to meet their lovers
As you claimed to have hurried to meet me
Climbing the stairs on what might be called the same legs
Darting quick glances of promise
Through biologically the same eyes
But refusing my hand when I reached for the hips
You must have lost in a careless moment since.

Naturally I will have no pity
And no more reason for anger.
I will marvel, though
At the handiwork of God, at the fact
That I could have spent sleepless nights on account of this
     body
Which we both thought was yours
A comparatively short time ago.

FOR MY SON

Your mother may understand this poem with her mind,
You will grow to understand it with your body.

You are a man and I am happy for you,
Your chest is bare but you will be hard to stab in the back.

In time you will learn: sex is the best cure,
The safest way past a woman leads through her.

(If you were a girl I would not know what to advise you,
You could be hurt coming and going: it is sad to be a girl.)

FIVE STANZAS ON PERFECTION

I will not be reduced to what I am
For I cannot quite return to the sea.
But naked in a circle of strangers
I have only been afraid of myself.

I am a cloud: I rain for the same reason
A tree grows or a cat stalks a mouse.
A cockroach can explain nine-tenths of me.
The rest sent Buddha into the wilderness.

I may only have to cut out one very small part
To attain perfection either way.
I have been exploring myself with a knife
I can do no more for the best of my friends.

Not something simple, my limbs or my glands
(Cripples and eunuchs still have narrow lips)
Nor is it primeval selfishness alone:
I have seen women and even children weep.

But maybe an impalpable dark plane
Such as some sleep: no ripple, sight or sound
Or meeting myself very suddenly
In a little-known part of any town.

MEMORIES

The room has four walls, the room is empty,
and there is nothing left in the room.
Around the room the house is dying
the way worlds die.
I lived here, I am told. I don't remember.

What I remember is nothing to speak of:
a summer perhaps, and a flow of streams.
Now I am tired. Elephants
sit on my dreams.

PRAYER

O God—no more cleverness—no love—I cannot see,
I am yours now to do unto me
As you do unto flowers,
For the darkest ruins of the loveliest castles in your own
time
Are held in the hands of your wingless angels
And human candles light your unending nights
And the brightness of your days is invisible
To my naked eyes.

WINDS

My rage sits like milk
Lukewarm in my mouth
I may yet kill someone
The north wind goes south.

I may have been alive
Long before my birth
I may not die for years
The south wind goes north.

I may have loved the most
Those I've hated the least
I may end up alone
The west wind goes east.

How much can I take
Put me to the test
I may surprise you all
The east wind goes west.

SIX STANZAS ON HOMESICKNESS

The Tower thought that I was alone
And placed himself squarely before me:
"*Now* what do you do?" he said
Happy, that I was not amused.

"I am with my friends," I murmured,
"Tower go away, go away.
You mean nothing to them at all.
This is something purely personal."

I closed my eyes, not that it helped.
"Tell them about me," the Tower sat down.
I was embarrassed for who would care
To bore his new friends with an old Tower.

"We were children together," I blushed.
"I can't turn him out, can I?" I whispered.
Unbidden shadows crossed the room
My friends looked at me with some concern.

"His first stones were laid in the tenth century,
He really is an interesting old Tower,
I saw him every day, going to school.
Maybe he has something important to tell."

But my apologies were all in vain
My friends' eyes grew cold and seemed to turn inward
And I thought Towers must mean more than friends
But then he left quietly, I never saw him since.

FIVE MORE LINES

I speak a language I have never learned,
I do not belong to any nation,
I hurl sharp poems at the world
And keep looking at the wounds in my skin
At their point of penetration.

SONG

I am thirty-one
Described as a man
I want to be alone
And it looks as though I am.

Coming from the tribe
In which angels abide
I always told the truth
When I thought I lied.

Now with features pretty
And with powers dark
I live in the city
That grows in my heart.

Wearing a braided tie,
Cheerful most of the day,
I write poems as I
Have almost nothing to say.

I own a fountain pen,
A car with bucket seats,
And share a young woman
With two dead-end streets.

This Saturday I will
Lean on her well-shaped thighs
Wondering how I'll feel
In 1985.

EIGHT LINES FOR A SCRIPT GIRL

I almost know you now. You are your name,
The substance of your skin, the movement of your eyes,
The line of your lips, the texture of your hair,
Your phone number, the colour of your voice.

You are your breasts' shape, the full length of your limbs,
You are your smile, your nailpolish, your dress.
Later I'll know you more. Still later
I'll know you even less.

from THE HAPPY HUNGRY MAN

"And is the hungry man not happy? for is
he not unfettered of the passions that
enslave us? or is his desire not capable of
fulfilment? and are the many mysteries
of Allah not reduced for him but to a
single one?"

—attributed to Dibil el Khuzai, c 800 ad

The happy hungry man believes in food
The happy homeless man believes in a home
The happy unloved man believes in love
I wouldn't mind believing in something myself.

Wakes up in a good mood one morning

Look at rocks
Rocks look back at you
Stare at water
Water stares
You can play endlessly
Dropping words one
by
one
Until you fill the pit of silence
Or adding up seconds
Until you reach the sum of time
You can also sit down and eat

Lie down and sleep
Stand up and whistle
There is the air to breathe in and fly through
There are hills to climb up and look down from
You can build houses too
And destroy them
Beget children
And sprinkle gasoline over their bodies
You can learn foreign languages
Dolce far niente
Arbeit macht frei
And take strange women for long walks
In beautiful afternoons
You can make up codes for your friends
Secret signals of sounds
From bars of indifferent music
You can broadcast your voice
And televise your face
Or grow very old and ugly
There is simply no end to all the things
You can do.

Walks through a park on his way to work

We all have
A bench in the park to reach
And some of us reach it.
I saw an old man this morning who did.
He seemed to be happy.

Green, black and brown were the predominant colours,
The sky threw in some blue, the clouds some white.
He himself was pink.

He held a stick in his hand, a safeguard of some sort
Against gravity, dogs, the universe,
The dangers of existence, his own buckling knees,
All known enemies inside and outside,
Even perhaps the Angel of Death.

Well, a stick is better than nothing.
He must have been eighty, he must have known
All fights are unequal
Otherwise how could there be victors?

Sitting among modest flowers
A kind of victor himself
He raised his eyes to follow my progress.

Tries to decide where to spend the night

Sleep only with strangers
    for strangers sleep in peace
And will be perfect hosts
    you being a perfect guest
May touch nothing of yours
    and you nothing of theirs
Except their outer skin
    And the coffee-pot in the morning.

Sleep only with strangers
    for they are open and kind
They know you are here today
    and gone tomorrow
If you carry away a little object
    they can spare it
If you leave one behind
    they can throw it out the next day.

Be a knock on the door
    a voice on the telephone
The promise of a postcard
    without a return address
Sleep only with strangers
    it is for you they reserve
Their freshest linen
    and their cleanest smile.

*Receives news of a friend who offended
a group of people in some way*

In the last room of his penthouse
Where he prudently withdrew when they started knocking
    on the door
He looked over his papers and thought of adding
One more line to a letter but nothing occurred to him
Then he barricaded his door so as to make it more difficult
For them to enter and when he put the heavy cabinet
In place he thought "Seven more seconds"
And he further thought "A second is a unit of time"
And finally "Well I did what I could."
But so did they and three minutes later

They reached the last room of his suite
It took them 45 seconds to open the door
(He thought it might take them 50)
They kicked the chairs aside and touched him with their
    hands
And he turned his head away and looked through the
    window
Far above the city he looked across the river
And he said "All this is very amusing"
And "I remember these mountains when they were
    molehills" he said
And he was about to say something else when they cut his
    throat.

Sits in a small craft approaching a landing strip

             I will resist
The temptation to lament
The passing of my youth, the loss
Of many certainties, the gain
Of two sorrows for each anger,

Instead I will note a little of the slow
Movement of objects along a slender
Line between the gently rising
Breasts of two firm hills across

The approaching land, the parting
Lips of a ravine, the erection
Of trees, the capricious glint
In the cold eyes of a nameless lake.

Darkness reserves
Each night
For its own purposes
The friendly cows
Cease their meanderings at eight
And leave their fenced-in fields of carnal pleasure
Indeed an evening's ride across the country
Often reveals on both sides of the highway
Cows going home
With slow and steady steps
We may assume
That once they reach their stables they will cast
A careless glance into their looking-glass
Before they sit
undress

and ruminate

Women don't travel in clubcars
Young and innocent women especially don't
Salesmen travel in clubcars
And junior executives who don't rate airplane tickets
And senior executives who do but have heart conditions
So the girl in this clubcar is sitting pretty
The conductor gives her his full attention
Causes a little table to be lowered beside her
And personally tenders her a glass of tomato juice
And stands by until the rim of the glass
Has safely found its way to her suspicious lips.
Meanwhile the train moves onward to Montreal

Ancient forests yield to its passing
One can hear the wheels whispering to the axles
Did you know we have a virgin in the clubcar?
Soon she will respond to the last call for lunch
A happy piece of salmon will sit in her plate
Which she may reward with half a gentle smile.

*Recalls lunching with an executive of
the Canadian Broadcasting Corporation*

Being
Vaguely upset by the fact
That even the very sparrows perish,
They pulled some strings, sent me on a mission.

I met God yesterday.
He sat on a sort of throne
We were both slightly embarrassed.
"I have no answers for you," he said finally.
I was relieved but tried not to show it.
I had no questions.

Lunches with a bug in the park

A snail
Has blown its wet horn
A soggy bug sits
The point of autumn escapes him
Why can't it be summer forever?

God pardons some
But they lead aimless lives,
Hear their names whispered at unexpected hours,
Their hearts beat visibly and their lovers
Fail to recognize them in the street at times.

They dare not be by themselves as they're always alone,
They tend to rise early but are usually late,
Their laughter seems too ready, their smile too remote
Indeed, it is better not to be forgiven.

Because God's mercy is colder than liquid air
And those he permits to punish themselves will learn
To envy the crosses and the crowns of thorn
The Father keeps for sons particularly dear.

Dials a number then changes his mind

My life is halfway over
And I still have no one to blame
I have not seen any monsters
Only some monstrous crimes.
Last night a girl tried to kill me
She said because of fear
But I've hunted the bluebird myself
And hunting is a ruthless affair.

                    Through some chance mutation
Poor G.J. has no organ to love with
The way he sees with his eyes
Tastes with his tongue
Thinks with his mind
Screws with his penis
Scratches and bites with his nails and teeth

But having the urge to love

He tries loving with his eyes
His teeth and nails
His mind   tongue   penis
And it still surprises him
That he's not quite satisfied.

She looked as though she had a secret
When we first met but she had none.
She lived in a flat on Cottingham Street,
My eyes were soft, her mouth was firm.

Later we drove in an open car
Around the country and we made
Love in the lake and I seem to recall
Drinking a bottle of champagne in her bed.

She looked as though she had no secret
After a year but she did have one.
It turned out to be the standard secret.
My eyes were cold, her mouth was drawn.

Now we haven't spoken for quite a while
My eyes are vague, her mouth seems lazy
We nod when we meet in the street, we smile
And we still share the same cleaning lady.

Gets angry at a meeting around 3 p.m.

The beasts are coming at you:
Destroy one beast.

Do not strike for humanity
Or as a warning.

Nevertheless
Destroy one beast.

If possible
Destroy one beast every day

For the same reason
That you drink a cup of coffee in the morning
Destroy one beast.

It is a pleasant thing to do.

Destroy one beast.

Moses and I
Must have climbed different mountains
Or must have been advised by a different god
For look at the writing on the stones in my hand:

It seems I may not respect my parents
Or my neighbour's right to the things he believes he owns
Or the lives of those I consider to be my enemies.

Before you begin to envy me
Remember only this:
My god's bidding is as remote from my nature
As your god's is from yours
And I find his commandments
As difficult to keep.

Why did I play a great many roles?
Why did I say words of a certain kind?
Why did I touch some of the breasts I touched?
I could go even further.

Yesterday—this was a minor thing—
I had lunch with a man I loathe.
I smiled at him, we talked of intimate matters.
I kept asking the waitress for more coffee.

We discussed his sex-life in some detail
And the role of a gold tooth in his lower jaw
And the time he really made it work
And, I said, let's have lunch again soon.

Of course, I remember actually risking my life
So that some fool would not think I was a coward,
But as I would do it any time again
I assume it was myself I wanted to impress.

But other things are harder to explain.
Why did I play a great many roles?
Why did I say words of a certain kind?
Why did I ask D.R. to lunch again?

A day will come and throw some light on it
Perhaps a day will come when I will *know* it
When that day comes perhaps it will all make sense
Then the day will come when it will not make the slightest
    difference.

□□□

Contemplates writing a film script

□□□

Outraged
        executives caught in air raids
Whimper in the most gratifying way

Conquering crews in capsized tanks
Burn for some time and grow very peaceful

Nor is it necessary to look for the spectacular:
Small tumours mollify malignant old women

The cunning Inca sacrifices his daughter
Because he understands the nature of his God

In a modestly optimistic fashion
I'm looking forward to the Last Judgement.

Hangs up after telling a woman on the telephone
at midnight that he will not live with her

We are happy tonight
With no hard news to tell
This autumn comes on time
The leaves are falling well

We have duly received a charge
We have duly tendered a bill
Closed what we had to close
Killed what we had to kill

Now we'll turn to the God
Whose commandments we keep
Kiss him   switch off the light
Undress and go to sleep

Makes a brief political statement
the next morning

I wish to be quite accurate.

This Imperial City is not dear to me:
I am not entertained by her circuses
Not impressed by her legions
And I do not adore
Her murderous immaculate gods.

The fire that is now visible
Even after sunrise
As it leaps from one suburban rooftop to the next
Does not take me by surprise
I will not need time
To gather my possessions
I have little desire to escape
And nowhere to escape to.

Some seem to take pleasure
In fanning the flames
And some think it right to do so
But I am not inclined to join them
Fires require no assistance.

Nor will I carry water for in all good conscience
I no more wish to see this city preserved than destroyed
City of slaves
City of gladiators
City of vestal virgins:
As all roads led to you for quite some time
For quite some time all roads will lead past you.

But unlike many
I have also been outside the gates
Marching with the armies of the barbarians
Exchanging love with them in their own language
And sleeping with my eyes open in their camps
And I am afraid.

I hereby give notice of my intention
To play my fiddle while Rome is burning.

He hitches a ride

One hundred miles:

He said he was coming along for the ride
If she didn't mind and she forgot to say no
And the summer was as friendly as a milkshake
And they rode across southern Ontario.

Two hundred miles:

In Buffalo they had coffee together
In Rochester they saw a smiling cop
In Marathon they tended to be quiet
In Syracuse his head was in her lap.

Three hundred miles:

They knew there was no point to their friendship
And quickly agreed not to pursue it further
He was on his way to a march through Manhattan
And she had to turn north at the Quebec border

Four hundred miles:

And anyway he knew her teeth were crooked
And anyway she found his face too hairy.
They nearly said goodbye, but on second thought he
        screwed her
On the New York State Thruway at Canajoharie.

It is reassuring
To spend part of a night
With an American girl.

Chances are she will not resemble
The leaders of her nation
In speech, figure or stance:

If she has imperialistic designs
She may draw you without a struggle
Into her sphere of influence.

Then you'll find her battledress
Fit for her private battles,
See not her battleships but hear her battlecries,
And melt (perhaps with a wistful smile)
Before the native napalm of her eyes.

But she'll seem to be prepared
To give as well as to accept
Some foreign aid

And by midnight or so
While the fires of her manifest destiny smoulder
You'll be all ready to slip across
The world's longest undefended border.

Next day he is forced to explain himself again

That's not the way
The world works.

You can't have a little food
A little money
A little love.

You can have much or nothing.
Much
Or nothing.

It makes no sense, yes.
There's no good reason for it, no.
So don't believe me, don't.
Say it's a passing mood.
Go on, ship your wheat to Asia,
Clear slums,
Redistribute wealth,
Rehabilitate prisoners,
Liberate the oppressed,
Educate the ignorant,
Construct a condition of justice.

But Asia won't be full until Europe goes hungry,
Slums will relocate themselves,
Wealth will find its own level: a slope,
Which it seeks with the physical force of water
And just as relentlessly
(But don't believe me)
Don't believe me when I say
                    The prisoners will become
                        jailkeepers
                    And the jailkeepers prisoners,
Don't believe me when I say
                    Your teachers will spread ignorance
                    And your scientists destruction.

"What would you have us do then?"

I would have you do exactly what you're doing:
Clear slums.
Educate the ignorant.
Liberate the oppressed.

Oh, it makes no sense, I admit.
There's no good reason for it, no.

Noticing

                              But I have elected to live
In legal separation from the world
Seen only
On rainy nights
Passing
With my lights out
Unknown
At any address
Matching
No description

from CITIES

MID-ATLANTIC

There are no cities here
but if I fly or float
for a length of time
in any direction
there will be a city.

In this sense
all cities meet here
and it is interesting to watch
the long shadow of Calcutta colliding
with the elegant narrow shades of Paris.

Here there is nothing
except much unstable air
ending in much unstable water
and a colour line where they meet.
Some travellers
have touched this line and lived to tell about it
but not many.

A LOVE POEM

May I tell you the truth?

When I dropped the sailboat's anchor
on the skull of the fish, its mouth opened wide
but only in agony, not supplication
as knowing no mercy pikes ask for none;
but fighting well for a body of fourteen
pounds of muscle and slippery green skin,
pulling a deep-keeled boat a quarter of a mile
surviving a keen slap of the paddle between the eyes,
a pair of pliers drawing a three-pronged hook
out of its gullet, taking whatever came with it,
and still biting the fisherman's finger with three rows
of immaculate teeth set in its dead jaws

may I tell you the truth—
cover girl   without eyelashes   lipstick
I saw your face.

TE DEUM ON YONGE STREET

In our own way
    in our own time
we praise the Lord everywhere
    te Deum laudamus
including this cocktail lounge
    mirrors   cathedral darkness
silver and ice
    green liquids swirling politely.
Behold a tall girl
    stained glass and marble
fabric of pale flesh
    structure of fine bones
confident stride and
    unconscious glory
in gloria Patris
    preparing her altar.
Sanctus sanctus sanctus Dominus
    holy holy holy Lord
Tibi omnes Angeli yes
    including this glass girl
marble bones eyes of ice
    proclaim unceasingly incessabili
coeli et terra heaven and earth
    pleni sunt majestatis gloriae tuae.
In fact how can one help praising the Lord
    if she can't help it tall girl
liquid air
    structure of fine bones
fabric of pale flesh
    blonde fibres

urban priestess
　　preparing her altar.
Marble girl　set out your tray and gimlets
　　praise God with your confident stride
a chorus of Apostles can do no more
　　nor a fellowship of the Prophets
nor yet a noble host of Martyrs:
　　Tu Rex gloriae, Christe,
judex crederis esse venturus
　　and perhaps you will be a lenient judge.
Help your servants　even the marble girl
　　we therefore pray　tuis famulis subveni
what else can we do now that we are created
　　and sit in cocktail lounges in crystal darkness
drinking green liquids politely　having been redeemed
　　quos pretioso sanguine　by your precious blood?
Through her perfect beauty we praise you O Lord
　　through her perfect beauty we cry for mercy
miserere nostri, Domine, miserere nostri
　　for how many years in your eternal universe
can a cocktail waitress wait　for how many years
　　before the fabric of her pale flesh crumbles
the stained glass of her eyes shatters　for how many years
　　in your world without end　saeculum et in saeculum
　　　　saeculi?
Accept her Lord　she magnifies you day by day
　　and keep her, like us, die isto sine peccato
if that is possible in her place in life
　　or at least let her sin be less than ours.
Behold　she serves us green liquids
　　marble and ice　pale flesh and fine bones
In te speravi, she whispers, non confundar in aeternum.
　　In te, Domine, in te speravi.

50

THE GIRLS OF WHITNEY HALL

Let me compose a simple prayer
    for things beyond recall,
embracing in the gentlest terms
    the girls of Whitney Hall.
No insight, bitterness or wit,
and soft enough to whisper it
    behind a private wall.

God, all they ever asked for was
    some perfect happiness:
marriage, orgasm, status, fame,
    free access and egress
for which in rooms they roamed a lot
talking of T.S. Eliot—
    why should life give them less?

The girls of Whitney Hall remain
    still pictures in a scene.
Textbooked, tennisballed, telephoned,
    progressive, poised and keen.
Married, fat, sucked up in a fog,
(one even coupled with a dog)
    unchanging and serene.

Please, God, give them wings to fly
　　and suntanned legs to walk;
poetry, sweet pain, requiems,
　　and small suburban talk.
Life insurance and ecstasy,
a blue Mercedes by the sea:
　　the flower and the stalk.

Because they are now 30 and
　　perceive the shadows fall;
because they've all held hands with Death
　　in brief ways, shy and small;
they're still desired by some men,
their hairdressers remember them,
O God absolve them if you can:
　　the girls of Whitney Hall.

LANDMARKS

After sixteen years I remember you
Ossington bus, O'Leary Avenue.

Perhaps gravity makes them loom so large
West Lodge, St. George Street, York garage.

Northcliffe backyard, where cops used to appear
after midnight to confiscate my beer

or Glenholm boarding house, five bucks a room,
whose dome languidly crumpled into doom

and bursting water pipes had drowned in steam
the ex-mate of a German submarine.

The beanery on Queen Street where a lame
girl first sat in my booth and asked my name.

Or long before, a metal winter night,
a funeral home's sign casting a light

flickering blue on grey December slush:
with cardboard trunks, torn clothes, needing a wash,

an evil-smelling strange boy, tall and thin,
had asked to spend the night. And god knows why

they took me in.

THE TELEVISION PRODUCER'S VISION

Mine is a heart that aspires
to Art made of electric wires
culled from the news,
uniquely common every story
with thousands having used before me
each word I use.

When I was young I meant to be a sculptor.
Now I sit middle-aged
before my glass and plastic altar.

In a soft wave of delicious self-pity
I find myself humming a little ditty:
    "A fisherman fishes
    a plumber plumbs,
    a good surgeon excises lumps,
    soldiers stand fast and cowards run,
    what have I done?"

I have done TV shows. The next will soon be on,
the mix-board hums with electricity,
the seventeen-foot boom extends its pecker,
the PA dons his cans, the switcher punches up
test-patterns on the colour monitor,
my script-girl comes with stopwatches and pencils
comfortable and all-familiar,
the intercom: the actors on the floor,
opening positions, dolly in,
the titles centre frame, okay, good luck—
I'm rolling tape at the top of the clock.

Mine is a heart that aspires
to Art made of electric wires,
selectively it admires
speakers of the truth and liars,
festivals, funeral pyres,
what amuses Hydra's head and
all that Hydra's head requires.

Only at times, through sounds the wires garble
I hear a statue speak:
a cold statue,
chiselled of blue-veined marble.

JARVIS STREET

The girl who's visiting me tonight
asks me to remember her to an executive
and next day I remember her.

"She's a loser,"
                    says the executive,
"let's go have lunch."

And that's that.
Except I seem to taste her in my Campari
and see her standing naked
at the window last night
with a tiny reflection
of the lights of the city in her eyes.

WHITE ANGLO-SAXON PROTESTANT IN CENTRAL PARK

I find the moonlight much too sharp
to hide my preference for pain.
Checkered shadows follow the lane
police advise me not to take across
        this lonely park
but I am set in my ways
the night is bright and my mood is dark.

Well, city, kill me if you can
having killed stronger men and better men.
I have a wallet, there's my watch to pawn,
        black man   white man
drug addicts, losers, whiners, victims come
        and take me on.

Indeed a man emerges from the bushes
but, on seeing me, turns and disappears.
Perhaps it is the aura of my breath
that makes the pale trees threatening and still,
for desperate as I have been for peace
        I am ready to kill.

I built this country. Shall I be the first
to yield what is best in it to the worst?
Why should I give in patiently? Jefferson's light

is programmed in computers.
The dreamers and the hidebound, Left or Right,
the envious, the weak, the slow of wit
have it reduced, transistorized and geared
to the requirements of human shit.

Are all lessons of history in vain?
All gifts of man to man painful and bitter?
Wealth by its nature choked in its own litter?
Ripe fruit a necessary poison to its root?
May I not seek a maximum of good,
and still retain a minimum of truth?

Men are equal in birth and death. Between
men are stupid and wise, they're kind and mean,
diligent/indolent, aggressive/shy,
tolerant/biased, timid/bold, dull/keen
the evidence of which we all have seen
        and seen fit to deny.

In every act there is a final choice
in spite of all complexities
between the silence and the voice.
Happiness not a right, but a pursuit:
we talk to God privately, and he makes
        reply to suit.

But even if I were alone
in not wanting my privacy defended
by a wire-tap on my telephone
        I'm not alone
in needing no more well-meaning policemen
to keep me from a lonely walk across
a city park of pale trees, slow and sane,

in which checkered shadows follow the lane
and shafts of moonlight far too sharp
to hide my preference for pain.

Pain, for I am not free. Cops and robbers
play games around me, both protected by
my tolerance and money. I have tried
far too long too many substitutes.
    I am not free
for I have valued comfort more than truth.
It is my city, I am not a stranger,
I myself could be danger if there's danger,
I myself could be murder if there's murder.
Not more policemen to escort me further,
Liberty, walk with me. I look to you again
    for my Law and Order.

CARNEGIE HALL

Because sadness is costly
and inadequate
                 and after a while
siege guns scale down to overtures

and finally our houses become ruins or monuments

also because of the hope that there will be a mind
to remember or to forget these cities
where bodies are even now being discharged
from hospitals and morgues
                         or admitted
into offices and jails and high society
                              This is
for the explorers of ephemera

This is for students of coded words
exhumers of graves and connoisseurs of explosions
collectors of potsherds
                     or readers
of the writing on the wall

This is trumpets for the ears of those whose hearing
has too become too subtle for loud music
it is kettledrums
                the rending
of foundations
                it is grenades
shattering granite

PARK AVENUE

When the middle-class girl and I
were finally lying side by side
on the white rug of her living room
in an expectant mood and naked

"What would you like me to do?" she whispered.

I admit her question surprised me,
it only seemed appropriate
for a virgin or a prostitute
and I did not think she was either.

In fact she turned out to be both.

LITERARY WIFE

Her blue veins run under white skin
and on her temples (where they don't)
she paints them on to denote
extreme sensitivity.

She wears her raw nerves on her sleeve,
complains that she's putty in the hands of her little boy
then dismisses him with steel-blue eyes
when he interrupts her *bon-mot*
and sends his father (the poet) to read him a bedtime story
preferably of angelic, long-suffering mothers.

She offers more tinned macaroni to her guests,
her specialty
on which she expects to be complimented
(and is, by her husband,
who has now returned from putting the boy to sleep
and is ready to play straight-man to her).
After dinner they will continue
collaborating on a novel:
he writing down her stream of consciousness
for a full share of the credits.

But for the time being she tells a story
of a famous writer's visit to their town
who it seems was much impressed with her looks and mind,
and sent her a book later, parts of which she enjoyed.
She also remembers his public reading well
because she was looking so radiantly young
they refused to serve her in a bar.

In passing she mentions her husband is ten years older than
  she.

What else can she tell us?
Michaelangelo's *David*
is a great work of art, and she herself said so
in a prizewinning essay in school;
then a look at her husband
sends him running
to fetch her watercolours.

WARSHIP ON THE THAMES
"In poetry there are neither big nations nor small . . ."
George Seferis

A poet and his lady gracefully accept
a leather-bound Russian edition of his book
from a peace-loving cultural attaché.

Small white hands hold cocktail glasses
all night long. Then like grey elephants
mansions of commerce march along the quay.

Suddenly under the deserted bridge
a claxon's blast warns of a slender
warship slicing the river in half.

The peace-loving poet carefully monitors
the braided water behind the twin screws.
Light naval guns point at his lady.

Academic eyes, sardonic, secure,
view the passing of the ship. A great navy:
a great agent for a great literature.

THE CENOTAPH

I don't feel like saying hello to you because I'm dead,
it took me a long time to die and now I mean to enjoy it.
Soon it will rain and you will stop blowing your trumpets,
and walk or drive home to your toiletbowls and teapots.

I approve of all this but I'm not interested any longer.
The bullet that will stop you is still in the making.
Perhaps the coal that will heat the furnace that will temper
     the steel
of which the weapon is styled that will enter your flesh
     has not yet been mined.

It is also possible that being less lucky than I was
you will die in your pyjamas instead of your boots,
surrounded by doctors who depend for their living on your
     kidney stones
and no schoolchildren will bring flowers for your graves.

Having known both, it seems to me that life ends in death
and perhaps a man could do worse than be killed by other
     men.
For there are those who die by water, by love, by going to
     the grocer,
by dull silver coins, by their own hands, or by their own
     bodies.

WOMAN IN EARLS COURT ROAD

He left her eight months ago
and she's quite happy.

She never thinks about him,
except one night in her bed
she touched him, held him,
dreaming she had wakened from a dream
in which he left her eight months ago.

It's been some time since she put his books
in a trunk in her cellar.
Before she closed the lid
she saw, but only for a moment,
his naked headless body.

Once in a while he passes her in the street,
eye-sockets full of sea-weed,
and tongues of blue flame rising,
for no reason, in his hair.

CAESAR IN LONDINIUM

"What was peculiar to Caesar will never be found in the things
Caesar had in common with a million other men."

Petru Dumitriu

In what way was Caesar different from other men?
Caesar dreamt that he possessed his mother
but many men dream such dreams,
I remember dreaming that I possessed my mother
and I am not Caesar.
In what way was Caesar different from other men?

In what way was Caesar different from other men?
His name has gone down in history
but many men's names have gone down in history,
history consists of men's names having gone down in it
and history is not Caesar.
In what way was Caesar different from other men?

We are told that Caesar the conqueror crossed the Rubicon
but Hitler conquered, and even I have crossed the Rubicon
alea jacta est at eighty miles along the Autostrada
but Hitler was not Caesar and we have already agreed
that I am not Caesar myself.
In what way was Caesar different from other men?

Of course Caesar was killed by (among others) the man
he loved as his son, but are not other men
killed by (among others) their sons, or by strangers
they love like sons, or by comrades-at-arms turning
their arms against their comrades?
In what way was Caesar, et cetera?

People say Caesar made a fool of himself over a girl
but many of us have Cleopatra in our closets
or at least an item of her clothing
and Caesar's face is not reflected in our mirrors.

In what way was Caesar different from other men?
Literature fails by drawing resemblances.
Psychology fails by seeking first causes.
Biology fails by concluding Caesar was a vertebrate.
And Jonas is puzzled.

OLD BAILEY

A thief loses a hand, a murderer
breaks on the wheel, mild justice puts the eyes
out of one merely demented,
but pray for those who offend the Lord God:
they have their wishes granted.

Oh bitter punishment, oh centre circle of hell,
they become kings, admirals, they win
the man or woman they covet,
nothing is spared them by gentle fate;
what their folly desires, they will have it.

And is there end to man's folly?   Is there one
not his own worst judge, or who having won
his poisonous prize, relented?
Pray for those who offend the Lord God,
they'll have their wishes granted.

OLYMPIC AIRLINES

A ripe woman, dark hair and darker eyes,
casts a single glance across the aisle.
Catching it, I throw it quickly back,
then we sit without a smile.

She is silent and I am silent too
but even our silences fail to meet
because I say nothing in English
and she says nothing in Greek.

CAFÉ MOZART

Soon
I am told
no one will read print
drink coffee from small cups
talk in complete sentences   but I
acting on this assumption
clean my glasses
sit quietly
observe this Danubian evening.

Light rain falls on dark stones.

Soon
I am told
no one will live in agreeable climates
it will be Arctic days or black sun
youthful and teeming and glass and spurting blood
naked activists with good teeth and blue bazookas
a new world: a new world
                              but here
a waiter in whose patent leather lifetime
psychoanalysis and the sewing machine
were introduced
                        brings me
a glass of water on a grey tin tray.

This of course is a marble table
in a café in a street in a city
more for suicides than conclusions

but still

a heartbreaking silver Mercedes
has just picked up a 5′8″ girl.

Soon
I am told
there will be no injustice
hermaphrodites will have equal rights
Asia will liberate Africa
rice will grow in the sea, old age
will be eliminated   though first
possibly
a few people

Yes   it seems   at first
a few people   But this is no news
in this particular street.

The rain becomes invisible.
I am exceptionally happy.

KÄRTNER STREET

There is something wrong with my eyes.

It is where it
begins
I am told
I am told   there are
elegant shops in this street
slim mannequins behind crystal windows
but all I see is blood
my ophthalmologist
has warned me
my literary friends have warned me
but even in my dreams I come upon
scenes of disaster
at ski resorts
cocktail parties
in glamorous towers where I try to live
meeting only handsome people
healthy people
wealthy people
all my life I have avoided hospitals
the waiting rooms of dentists
urologists
social workers
the meeting halls of the hopeful
the hopeless
rushhour streets
the subways of this world
but the composed couplets in which I speak
to which I exclusively

allow myself to listen
echo of grief
remorse   mourning
grief
remorse and
why is this stylish lady calling for help?

LADY ON THE AVENUE OF THE VIRGIN MARY

In this strange world of outer space
    vulnerable and small
she calls for her lover because
    who else is there to call?

Her nights are cold, her days are dry,
    her planets far away,
she says her love will never die,
    what else is there to say?

In this strange world of outer space
    she has no one but you:
love her. Learn to see her ways
    from her point of view.

Be faithful to her, and she'll cut
    the core out of your heart;
in one sense it is unfair but
    who else is there to hurt?

KUNSTHISTORISCHES MUSEUM

For whose sake shall I lie about you
oxhide-belted
double-edged
single-minded
infantry sabre?

In the end
it is not lovers   friends   museums
it is you.

I return to you
I always return to you
from those other rooms   paintings
golden salt cellars
gobelins   crystals   clocks
I return to you.

From the Emperor's
hundred-and-twenty diamond
teaspoons I return to you.

I love my brother,
reads the inscription.
My sword loves me.

Hard metal   cold metal
unfashionable metal
whosoever lived by you
perished by you:
not by flaccid thoughts

barbed-wire words
fisheyed compassion: by you
straight metal sweet metal.

The man who had you by his side
had one certain protector. If he is dead
he is not likely to be more dead
than a lover of peace.

AIR RAID RHYMES

A child, very shy:
dark death, I wondered, bitter death,
painful death, why?
What is it, who
makes it, how does it come about,
is it true?
Was there someone, perhaps a survivor,
who knew?

A bomb, my teacher said,
weighs fifty pounds.
During class, from hand to hand,
a bit of shrapnel made the rounds.
Dark death, I wondered, bitter death,
painful death, why?
What is it, who
makes it, how does it come about,
is it a lie?

When walls collapsed, the bodies
were covered with burlap sheets.
Air raids were fun, school was out early,
we were playing in the streets.
I remember being a siren: I screamed,
the others ran.
I dived like a plane, like a bomb I exploded,
learning to be a man.

Wardens were digging up cellars,
the dead were laid in a row,
gas-mains burned
with a beautiful blue flame:
I was longing to know, to know.
Dark death, I wondered, bitter death,
painful death, what is it you feel?
But the faces were closed and secretive,
rigid, black, shrivelled, and sealed.

I woke at dawn, shivering, I think my
father was watching silver darts
trailing white smoke in a pink sky.
Go to bed,
father said,
this is not an alert only a warning:
it's Warsaw they're bombing this morning.
Tell you what we'll do,
we'll put it to music for you:
"Not an alert, it's only a warning,
it's Warsaw they're bombing this morning."

My father playing the piano,
grey puffs of ack-ack sprouting in the sky,
dark death, I wondered, bitter death,
is it a game or a lie?
What is it, who
makes it, how does it come about, why?

When the sirens started up again
some bombs, my teacher said,
weighed fifty pounds;
spilling the ink, watching the purple stain.
I weighed a hundred pounds: would I be death,

if I dropped on a city from a plane?
Would I be dark, would I be bitter death,
would I be pain?
Would I be faces, cold and black and sealed,
if I were Death itself, what would I feel?

And growing silver wings, I rose, I flew,
I soared across the city, sweet and shy,
becoming Death, having no wish to die,
having no patience with my father's song,
being in air raids on the ground was wrong
and while good boys took shelter with the rest,
I rained phosphorus bombs on Budapest.

GOING HOME

Where did Imogene the spider
        disappear to? Her world
was made of little particles. A landmine
        is buried in the garden.
Winepress, Turkish tobacco, dust.
        Uncle's bicycle, bleeding.
Remember the goldfish? The cat got it,
        a shrapnel got the cat.
Cook's dog, playful, chasing his own tail,
        he used to run around
this tree, the tree they later hanged cook from.
        They thought she was someone else.
Come, look at the library. Remember?
        No more books, a day care centre
first, then an interrogation chamber,
        now it is just a room.
Oh, we're fine. Your cousins too,
        we pick cherries, the lake
is much the same. The tower, no. The tower,
        the old tower is gone.

AIRPORT

He had been trailing her for a week.

In and out of taxis,
receptions,
officials saying "Madame
Minister will be late this morning,"
shaving quickly in hotels with red stars,
running out of money,
pressing the one decent suit
under the mattress,
memorizing the words,
hoping
to be alone with her
he, a simple worker,
to tell her everything
to make her listen.

Then the September day
knowing it would be that day
or never.

At the airport
her plane waiting, a scheduled flight,
Madame Minister being
fifteen minutes late, arriving finally,
smile, immaculate dress,
still attractive, dark hair, small Party badge.

Only one official
following her along the corridor.

The face a mask,
no smile now, no reporters,
jet-engines whining, gloves
carried in one hand,
only ten paces away.

Only five paces away,
and so much to say
after such a long time:
knowing that every word had to count
to make her stop
                              stop, listen to him
a simple worker
before the secretaries came
before the jetplane flew off
before

He knew he had to penetrate her heart
and feared words might not do it.
He used a long thin blade.

HOTEL ROYAL, 1970

The April wind is gentle.
The socialist sky is blue.
Our limousine is waiting.

My friend the film director pans toward me
and stops with his innocent eyes in extreme close-up.
He informs me he's happy.

He is happy in a happy country,
free, creative, and soon he will drive
to his island retreat in his East German car.
He dollies back for a final goodbye
and fades out slowly.

The April wind is gentle
the socialist sky is blue
the limousine waits patiently.

A shabby woman steps into the frame,
informs me she has not eaten for three days
and asks me for five *forints*.

I wave at my friend and smile,
and give the woman three *forints*,
and get into my limousine.

They are probably both lying
and I've become too old to chase after
the whore of truth in strange cities.

EMILE X, STUDENT REVOLUTIONARY, KILIAN BARRACKS

Fit for long walks & quiet words,
    yellow autumn day;
"Without some blood this fucking state
    will not wither away.

Perhaps it's wiser to be wise
    patient & discreet,
but soak some rags in gasoline,
    set fire to your street.

Bullets punch holes in two-bit whores
    bare-assed in defence,
this time the magic's in your guns
    & not in making sense.

Sweet children it is battle time:
    on your feet & fight,
good reason may make you again
    circumspect and polite

but rise up first & burn the shit
    right out of the pricks
who drive tanks on your fathers' land
    in nineteen fifty-six."

EMILE X, STUDENT REVOLUTIONARY, CITY HOSPITAL MORGUE

1.

I'm a flame: a process not a structure.
Growing from match to paper to wall to roof
growing from house to houses to street to town
I have shape, height and bulk only to deceive those
who think they know my limits.

I don't mean to boast: a child's breath blows me out
and I retreat hissing from a bucket of water;
but I won't be cut down to size, defined,
contained, dismissed: I'm a flame, I'm alive,
I can't be measured in inches or weighed in carats,
I flare up or die down; celluloid
transports me in a flash; oil
feeds me; timber
preserves me; I burn, therefore I am.

Of course I have often been harnessed
ever since Prometheus, for I'm strong
yet less trouble than elephants or horses,
and willing to serve for I'm above service;
like all things, I don't know right from wrong
and I exist only to be, like all things.

Men have cursed me and worshipped me.
I have warmed them and I have killed them,
as I've warmed or killed their enemies.
No one has ever stopped me. If I'm stopped I disappear.

I go underground. Everything combustible
hides me forever. I'm a flame:
a process not a structure.

2.

I died (to use a conventional term)
at six this afternoon, of complications
after a steel fragment lodged in the left
upper part of my lung. The grenade was fired
by an enemy of the revolution
using a grenade launcher, late last night.
As it was dark and things were confused
it is also possible that a friend of the revolution
launched the actual grenade. I mention this in brackets:
whoever pulled the trigger, I was killed
by the enemy.

I'm a flame: a process not a structure.
If you capture me you have to feed me,
if you set me free I look after myself.
Only an enemy of the revolution,
an unthinking, wishful policeman
would try to put me out with bullets or grenades.

3.

I address these remarks to you because you are a friend
and have come to look at me in the City Hospital Morgue
where like a long white flame with a purple tip
I'm going through the invisible motions of rigor mortis
and maybe only you know that I'm alive.

For a while I will sleep now as flames sleep
in solid blocks of wood, electric wires,

plastic fibres and sheets of aluminum.
I will sleep as gasoline sleeps in steel barrels,
dynamite sticks in warehouses, as sound sleeps
in jet engines, as thunder sleeps
in tumulescent clouds above the Great Lakes.

I will not be dismantled or put out: you know me,
I'm a flame: a process not a structure.
Growing from match to paper to wall to roof
growing from house to houses to street to town
from good to better to bad to worse
from love to malice to pain to compassion
from peace to justice to injustice to war
I burn, for burning is my business.

I'm a flame: a process not a structure.
Walk with me to the cemetery. In time
I'll walk with you.

NEW POEMS

INSCRIPTION

Signals   signals
behold   from the outer darkness
another flash of light:
Cor mea clavis

The heart is my key
(to good & evil, no doubt)
the key is my heart

Breakfasted on bones
wiped my mouth with
my best friend's hand
dumped my lover   my lover
into the dustbin—
the world is safe:
Cor mea clavis

The arbiter   the judge
inside my chest   my head
my conscience   my
categorical imperative
my one-to-oneness with God
(no moderator: no moderation)
my honesty   my faith
gut-feeling   amygdala
by any other name:
Cor mea clavis

It opens & locks any door
such is the key of my heart
a skeleton-key

Looks perfect on a crest
in a blue field   across
a sinister bar & under
the tip of a sword

JOAN ESTELLE AND THE MAGICIAN

1.

She was Joan Estelle   an A-minor person
who walked curiously sideways & never
quite in front of her own private shadow or behind it
like other people

2.

She was Joan Estelle   who when she appeared a dark-
blue cloud followed her uptown
from the foot of Bay Street & no one
knew why

3.

Acquaintances swore it was not staged & no
special effects for thunder & no wind-
machine to make her dark hair billow
& her skirt cling to her thighs

4.

They said no she did not
employ God as a gaffer & the sun
backlit her at the right dramatic instant
just by coincidence

5.

She was Joan Estelle   & it so happened that things
simply happened to her that normally never

happened to other people who had no dark-
blue clouds over their heads & were not
A-minor persons & no thunder
announced their presence & no wind
played in their hair

6.

For she could stir a pound of sugar & two
eggs into her milkshake & wear a D-cup & draw
every eye to herself crossing a room & still remain
quite insubstantial

7.

And many coveted Joan Estelle & some were angry
& more than one advised others to stay
away from her but they couldn't because
they clearly saw her passing without being certain
they had seen her pass

8.

And it happened that Joan Estelle being like air
& being like water but mainly being
like herself came to the city
& the city said all right I'll throw her up high
but maybe I won't catch her

9.

Maybe I won't catch her said the city
having thrown up high many people but
having caught only a few & some having
been like air & some like water & many
just like Joan Estelle

10.

For people with dark-blue clouds over their heads
were no news to the city & the city had heard
noises like thunder breaking at the right
dramatic instant many times before
& it would take a lot of walking sideways
parallel to one's own private shadow
to impress the city

11.

But there were no signs of course & Joan Estelle had
no inkling in restaurants or boutiques or tennis courts
or go-carts or TV studios or theatres or looking
at herself on the front cover of Eaton's
catalogue of the city's strategy

12.

And let it be said if she had had an inkling she
wouldn't have cared for she was nothing
if not daring

13.

She was Joan Estelle   an A-minor person
who came to see & conquer in a vague &
insubstantial way & would never settle
like people of no wind & no thunder & no private shadows
for mere survival

14.

And let it be said if she knew nothing she knew
at least this   To survive only to survive
is not to survive much

15.

She was Joan Estelle   & if the city didn't like it
the city could go sink & of course the city did not
but smiled & retreated & clicked its cameras in
admiration & offered her bone china & Gucci bags
& bided its time

16.

Meanwhile Joan Estelle was saying NO to men
& said it so often it became a habit
& would say NO when someone asked her the time of day
& NO to a second helping of ice cream &
luckily no man asked her to please breathe
because she would have had to shake her head
NO & suffocate

17.

For she who is at any given moment
backlit by the sun does not ask to be loved
& tenderness is an anathema for an A-
minor person

18.

And kindness causes her pain & gifts
nauseate her & she cannot help
stepping on those who prostrate themselves
before her feet

19.

And after she had broken everyone who came near her
& some who tried to stay away Joan Estelle said

who oh who will please break *me* & the city
listened & answered   a h a

20.

A h a   answered the city as she walked uptown
& a dark-blue cloud followed her from the
foot of Bay Street & everyone wondered why
& many coveted her & some were angry &
more than one advised others to stay the hell
away from Joan Estelle

21.

But having thrown her up high said the city now
she's finally falling & maybe
no one will catch her

22.

Maybe no one will catch her said the city
as it observed her running from person to
person begging them to please please break her
but they couldn't

23.

And it was clear if no one could Joan Estelle
might finally break herself for she had
her own private shadow & could not exist
without being broken but in the nature of things
could hardly go on existing broken
to pieces either

24.

It was at this precise moment when all seemed lost
that Joan Estelle ran into the magician who
stood on the corner of Bloor & Avenue Road
having just come from a different century naked
except for a watch & an ebony cane

25.

And being uncertain what he was doing here & where he
      was
going next he listened as Joan Estelle begged him
to break her at which he recognized
an A-minor person

26.

And having nothing better to do & knowing all
about people whose presence is often
announced by thunder & dark-blue clouds
hover above their heads but still they look
quite insubstantial

27.

He glanced at his watch which showed Toronto time
& when the hands stood at half past ten
he broke Joan Estelle to pieces but being a magician
he put her together again.

FATHER: A PORTRAIT

He dreamed at his clavier and counted his gold,
and knew instinctively it's futile
as is reading Goethe or growing old
or arguing with a crocodile,

but he took it for granted for some reason
that posterity's a valid forum,
for everything there's a season,
and Adolf Hitler would die before him.

He promised my mother, it appears,
that a Mediterranean villa
awaits the prudent man who steers
a course between Charybdis and Scylla.

But readers of Goethe learn to accept
a quirk of the world no gold can redeem:
that dreamers wreck their ships on a fact
and prudent men, on a dream.

FOOTNOTE ON THE NEWS

Terrorists threaten to dynamite
a planeload of civilians, unless.
Commandos land and kill the terrorists.

Reactions are predictable:
The United States congratulates, etc.,
the Soviet Union condemns, etc.

Canada is silent.

Explains an official: To exercise
moral leadership in the world we must
observe strict neutrality
between good and evil.

NOCTURNAL

Oh how we entered
    dear madame dear
a temple well tempered
    oh how we entered.
Glances held four beats full
slim fingers sculptured slim
      icons with sainted
      gestures newly painted
cool nipples textured cool
all centres centered:
                       lean
invisible man: keen
woman, heads turning slowly, in
we went, skin
brushing against skin,
    oh how we entered, a drop
at a time, a stop
after each note
a flute
in his crushed velvet suit
a harp,
strings taut in her smart
Missoni coat
    but now a little fear
    strikes the hammerklavier
where, how much, through what jumbles,
snakes, bones, trinkets, truth-serums, iron maidens,
whose nails
across whose eye
for that matter how soon or why:

Perhaps a lapse
perhaps a lapse again, perhaps a lie?
    Dear madame dear
with all centres centered
how well tempered
      is the temple we entered?
Now for a last brilliant passage
slim fingers on the keyboard of her spine
his eyes   crushed velvet   blue
      c'est tout.

FROM THE BOOK OF AL-MAARI

Burning stakes blossom from the footsteps of Redeemers;
the Koran fashions daggers carried by true believers;
the atheist has faith in what his eyes disclose,
the Sufi, what he sees when both his eyes are closed.
It is a Buddhist doctrine that all doctrines must fail;
the Hebrew knows nothing in exquisite detail;
the Brahmin fears the risk which in his next life he runs;
the hedonist trembles, for his life comes only once
and briefly. In the great insane asylum
of this revolving earth chaos creates the rules.
There are believing and unbelieving fools.

(after George Faludy)

THE POET ABU NUWAS TO HARUN AL-RASHID

With knees drawn to my chin, like a grasshopper,
I lie in my cell on an iron rail.
Remember me, great Caliph, do not suffer
your servant Abu Nuwas to perish in jail.

Forgive my transgressions. The holy law,
the Koran has become my only joy.
I hold it as I used to hold, with awe,
the silken backside of a growing boy.

(after George Faludy)

IBN AMAR THE ANDALUSIAN, 1080 A.D.

The parks, the nights, the naked bodies' blur,
the fountains, and the library of course,
the olivetrees, the minarets, the myrrh,
the honeyed scent of joy without remorse.
He had a fair sword and a jet-black horse.
In pride he wrote this, because it was clear
that all within the high walls of Seville
worshipped and quoted him, the grand Vizier:

"I am Amar. The fame of my verse flies
over the mountains and the western sea
and from the south the desert wind replies
only a fool is ignorant of me.
A golden lizard on a golden disc,
if I slither from the lewd lips of a boy
in the eager ear of an odalisque
she leaves her master and becomes my toy.
Nor will this change after my body lies
under my obelisk."

He was cheerful and happier than I
for when on Spanish domes the arabesque
loosened and fell, he never questioned why,
or why people grew flabby and grotesque,
and did not sense the fabric's fading dye
or in his own tunic the broken thread,
the fountains of the city running dry,
he did not taste the filth inside his bread
or see the boys who knew his poems die
or view the burning library with dread.

Brave and clever, he failed to note the fact
that faith's no help, nor wit, courage, or dagger,
that no philosophy will resurrect
a culture, once it collapses forever.

(after George Faludy)

FRENCH INTELLECTUALS, 1946

Look at these men of pale and intent faces,
hear these women of no secular graces,
in this land they live and prosper like weeds after a rain.
They earn their living by singing the praises
of Russia, where they'd only earn a bullet in the brain.

(after George Faludy)

THE LETTER
with which Walafridus Strabo submitted his Book on Horticulture
to Grimaldus, the Abbot of Gallen, around 830 A.D.

The book my messenger leaves at your gate
is modest for a gift, not in accord
with the merits of a spirit as ornate
as yours is, O my father in the Lord.
But it comes from a follower in the faith
whose eyes even now, while he marks these dots,
behold you in a rockgarden beneath
a small tree bearing yellow apricots
surrounded by the offsprings of your soul,
your family, disciples, casting lots
to gather for his pleasure pale-green peaches
on whose white beard the stars of which he teaches
throw showerheads of light through tiny slots
under the autumn's ornamental glass.
There, in that garden, gentle father, gazing
over the irises and tigergrass,
advanced in age but in strength still amazing,
untouched by ill-health, sloth, or gluttony,
read—which I boldly send you for appraising—
my brief commentary on botany.
Ponder it deeply, my modest creation,
tender me about it no lenient lies,
castigate its faults for my edification,
but if it merits some favour in your eyes
extol its virtues, O voice that fills the land
with tones of ringing brass in major keys,
for which may Christ place in your ancient hand
the olive branch of His eternal peace.

(after George Faludy)

108

AFTERWORD

I feel as though I play Coleridge to George's Wordsworth. In raw material, modulation and voice, we are at opposite ends of the spectrum. No one is better than George Jonas at taking the world around us in its populous dimensions and allowing its facets to reveal unknown lights.

The power of his verse on others was best illustrated to me back in the late sixties while on a reading tour. In those days, one usually got roped into lecturing to students at American universities about Canadian literature. George had given me a manuscript copy of *The Happy Hungry Man*. Instead of lecturing, I read George's work. At Loyola, in New Orleans, there was so much excitement about his work and so many questions about the man, I was made to feel that I was part of a Canadian conspiracy to keep his work a secret.

Later at the University of British Columbia, one hundred and sixty-nine copies of the same book sold at a single reading. Dennis Lee was then his publisher and thought I was daft for suggesting he send out so many books. I told Dennis I had a well-educated hunch.

For a quarter of a century George and I have been guiding one another through our respective wildernesses, entertaining one another, shocking friends by reading one another's work at performances, riding motorcycles—far less than we wished—getting into as much mischief as we could together, and chuckling at a world we have agreed is tragic but not serious.

For a quarter of a century I have tried to lure George to the west coast, and he has assured me I would soon adapt to living in Toronto and come to love it.

We once entered into a plan that he would bike from Toronto and I from Vancouver and meet half-way. Then there was a pause on both ends of the phone as we realized the meeting point would not be ideal motorcycle country.

George did not question my judgement in middle-age at becoming a prison guard nor at my climbing mountains. It makes perfect sense to me that, in his fifties, he races at Daytona with bi-focals.

It seems fate that we will dwell in our separate jungles. *The East Wind Blows West.* The west wind blows east. And we endure.

Jonas has long been my favorite poet writing in English. That our friendship has remained invincible this long time is simply a bonus.

It has been much too long since a book of his verse has been available. It has been a privilege to help bring this "new and selected" into print.

J. Michael Yates
Squamish, 1992